Archaeology

WARWICK PRESS

Contents

Editorial

Authors
Jean Cooke
David Heidenstam
Christopher Maynard
Theodore Rowland-Entwistle

Editor
Jennifer Justice

Left top: Volunteers at a "dig". Center: Portico at an entrance to the Palace of Knossos in Crete, partly reconstructed. Bottom: A diver raises an amphora from an old wreck.

Published by Warwick Press, 730 Fifth Avenue, New York, New York 10019.

First published in Great Britain by Sampson Low in 1976.

Copyright © 1976 by Grisewood & Dempsey Ltd.

Printed in Great Britain by Purnell and Sons Ltd., Paulton (Avon) and London.

6 5 4 3 2 1

Library of Congress Catalog Card No. 76-45482

ISBN 0-531-09076-0
ISBN 0-531-09051-5 lib. bdg.

Archaeology

"The archaeologist," said Sir Mortimer Wheeler, "is not digging up *things*, he is digging up *people*." This perhaps sums up the great change from the early days of collectors and scholars. Today's archaeologist sifts the very soil in an attempt to piece together the lives of people who may have lived thousands of years ago. In the early days much valuable evidence was destroyed through haphazard digging. Today the careful work of the archaeological team ensures that nothing is overlooked. Even a garbage pit can help to reveal how people lived.

Archaeology tells the story of the men who have gone in search of the past. It tells, too, of the famous discoveries that they made. Schliemann and Troy, Carter and Tutankhamun, Evans and Knossos are well known. Less is known about the hours and years of patient, sometimes boring work needed for uncovering less dramatic but no less valuable sites. Archaeology is still a young study. But bit by bit, archaeologists are helping to fill in the pieces of the fascinating jigsaw of human history.

Above: Carved ivory warrior in a helmet covered with tusks, as described by Homer, found at Mycenae. Below: Iron Age burial in Denmark. This woman had been buried with her jewelry.

Digging up the Past

Archaeology began as a treasure hunt. Today men study every clue to the past to piece together the history of civilization.

Archaeology is the scientific study of all the remains of past human life, from huge buildings to the homeliest pin. It can be called a branch of history, though its "records" are in stone, brick, bone, metal, or clay. The archaeologist is in a sense a detective, sifting and sorting the "clues" of history. His clues are often more reliable than written records. But he often needs scientific help to understand them.

Many of the exciting stories of archaeology are well known: Howard Carter's discovery of the steps down to the rich tomb of Tutankhamun; the tiny seals that led Sir Arthur Evans to the Minoan palace at Knossos; the legends of Homer that inspired Heinrich Schliemann to unearth the ancient cities of Troy and Mycenae. Less well known are the hours, months, and years of patient, painstaking work that go into uncovering any archaeological site.

The first sites to attract archaeologists were those that have remained above ground through the centuries. One was the Forum at Rome (below).

From collector to scholar

Archaeology can be traced back to the Renaissance, the time when a rebirth of interest in the ancient world led people to collect old statues from Greece and Italy. Many of these formed the start of the collections of the large museums of Europe, like the Louvre in Paris and the British Museum in London.

Some of the men who first came to see ancient sites were only interested in what they could take away with them. Others visited old ruins out of simple curiosity. They wrote descriptions of the ruins and made wild guesses about the people who had built them. The true pioneers of archaeology were men like Thomas Jefferson and General Augustus Lane-Fox Pitt-Rivers. Both faithfully measured and recorded even the tiniest details of their finds. Archaeology today is helped by science and modern tools. But it follows the same principle: nothing, however seemingly trivial, must be overlooked in uncovering a site. Detailed records are of the utmost importance.

Pazyryk Valley

Kul-Oba

R. Tigris

R. Euphrates

Nineveh

Megiddo
Jerusalem

Babylon

Ur

Persepolis

Mohenjo-Daro

R. Indus

Harappa

Man-Ch'eng

Archaeology today

Early archaeologists by mistake destroyed valuable evidence in their diggings. Even today sites threatened by new roads or buildings are often dug up hurriedly, and information is lost. But archaeologists have learned to dig in a methodical way. Every find is carefully recorded in position before being removed. Even the earth dug out may be analyzed to separate once-living matter from clay and stone. From important clues like seeds and bone we can picture the surroundings of people who lived several thousand years ago.

Science has come to the aid of the archaeologist in other ways. Radioactive carbon-14, present in all plant and animal matter, is used in dating finds and sites. Infrared and X-ray photography can show up designs under the rotted surface of a bronze bowl. Aerial photography has revealed the remains of early civilizations that were not visible from the ground. Cameras have been lowered into underground tombs to photograph paintings that might have been destroyed if dug up. Film also shows if the tombs are worth opening.

Archaeology today is a matter for experts. But they are often hampered by lack of time and money.

Some famous archaeological sites in Europe, North Africa and Asia.

A stone carving of a mythical beast at Persepolis, an ancient capital of Persia.

A print from a book of 1777 shows gentlemen in the diggings at Pompeii. Workmen wheel off treasures. These early digs were for unearthing statues, not revealing the past life of a Roman town.

Pioneers

Curiosity and the urge to collect led many early archaeologists to explore old ruins.

We know that King Nabonidus of Babylon (555–538 BC) restored the Ziggurat of Ur some 1500 years after this stepped pyramid had been built. He left a note recording his deed. Some might call him the first archaeologist. But the story of serious archaeology really begins much later. As recently as 200 years ago princes collected ancient statues for pleasure, not to learn about life in the past. But ideas were soon to change.

The antiquaries

In 17th-century England, men began to be interested in periods of the past for which there was little or no written history. A new sort of scholar appeared – the antiquary, a collector of old relics.

One of these antiquaries was John Aubrey (1626–1697). He is remembered today for his *Brief Lives* of famous men, which are amusing but full of errors. But as an early "field archaeologist" he did much work of value. For instance he described 56 strange holes surrounding the stone circle at Stonehenge. Modern archaeologists were able to find these so-called Aubrey holes at once from his notes.

Aubrey guessed that Stonehenge had been built before the Romans came. But he wrongly called it a temple of the Druids. The Druids were the priests described by Julius Caesar – the first Roman to invade Britain. Aubrey thought Druids "two or three degrees

John Aubrey was called "maggotty-headed," but his seething curiosity led to some good archaeological field work.

"Druidomania" marked the first wave of interest in the non-classical past. This 17th-century Dutch print shows a Druid and priestess surrounded by victims of bloodthirsty sacrifice.

THE ELGIN MARBLES

The biggest grab of the collecting period involved the Elgin Marbles. In 1799 Lord Elgin went to Turkey as British Ambassador. Turkey then ruled Greece. There Lord Elgin found the famous Parthenon temple half ruined. Elgin decided to rescue its sculptures. The beautiful "Elgin Marbles" were sent to Britain, and displayed in 1807. Eventually they passed into the British Museum, where they still remain.

The British Museum's Elgin Room in 1819. Famous men view the Greek sculptures.

less savage than the Americans." (He meant Red Indians).

William Stukeley (1687–1765) took quite a different approach. Stukeley published detailed accounts of the stone circles and other ancient structures of Britain. He was filled with the mistaken idea that the Druids had the perfect religion. But many of his drawings of old monuments are very accurate. His work marked the beginning of interest in pre-Roman civilizations.

The age of travel

In the late 17th century began the great age of travel. Beautifully printed books picturing the remains of ancient civilizations began to appear. By the mid-18th century no gentleman's education was complete unless he had made the "Grand Tour" of Europe, with a private teacher. Most of these wealthy young men brought home relics of the past. Men began to dig in search of the past. But at first, the motive was simply plunder.

One honorable exception to the treasure hunters was Thomas Jefferson, later to become third President of the USA. In 1784 Jefferson dug up an Indian grave site in Virginia. He did it with the care and precise observation that was not to be common until 100 years later.

Most of the articles dug up by the early excavators, or carried off by "Grand Tourists," were seen only as valuable works of art. Their owners ignored any story they might be able to tell about the past. But at least they were kept in collections, not melted down for their precious metals. And museums were set up with some idea of keeping the treasures of the past for the benefit of all. Slowly the modern idea of history – and thus archaeology – began to grow.

Thomas Jefferson, a great statesman and a pioneer of planned archaeology.

One of many books that excited interest in ancient civilizations was Jean Chardin's description of Persia, published in 1711. This picture from the book shows the ruins of Persepolis.

Secrets of the Pyramids

Napoleon's scholars stirred new interest in the statues and buildings of Ancient Egypt.

A French army stood beneath the Pyramids of Giza. The soldiers sweated in their blue uniforms under the hot Egyptian sun. Before them stood their general, a small man with a harsh voice and sharp eyes. Waving one hand towards the pyramids, he said: "Soldiers, forty centuries are looking down upon you!"

In this way the great general Napoleon Bonaparte began the archaeological exploration of Ancient Egypt.

Napoleon actually failed to capture the country. But the scholars he brought with him learned much about its past glory.

The riddle of the Sphinx

Among Napoleon's experts was a 51-year-old artist and archaeologist, Baron Dominique Denon. His many drawings of the ruins he saw appeared in a book published from 1809 onwards. Among Denon's drawings was the head of the Sphinx. The rest of the huge statue was buried in sand. We now know it has the body of a lion and the head of Pharaoh (King) Khafre. Khafre built the second largest pyramid.

Under the direction of Denon and his friends, the French collected all the old relics they could, and put them in the Egyptian Institute in Cairo. Probably they planned to take many of them to France. But Napoleon's defeat in Egypt in 1801 meant that his Egyptian finds ended up in British hands.

Napoleon and his scientists were puzzled by the Sphinx, and even more by the pyramids. More than 2000 years ago a Greek poet, Antipater of Sidon, placed

Napoleon's expedition to Egypt included a number of surveyors and engineers. Their findings awakened great interest in ancient Egypt.

the pyramids at the head of a list of the Seven Wonders of the World. These giant stone structures near Cairo, are the only "wonders" that survive.

In Napoleon's time people knew that the largest of the pyramids, the Pyramid of Pharaoh Khufu (Cheops) had rooms hidden deep within it. One had been made as a burial place for the pharaoh. Khufu reigned from about 2590 BC to 2567 BC. An old story told that 100,000 slaves had worked 20 years to build his tomb, using 2,300,000 blocks of stone each weighing about $2\frac{1}{2}$ tons. The entrance was skillfully hidden, because the pharaohs feared grave robbers. In fact, the way into the second pyramid, that of Pharaoh Khafre (Chephren), was so well

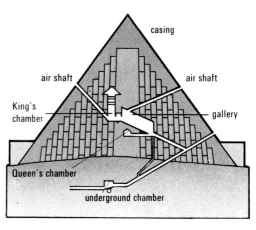

hidden that many people thought it was a solid structure. It took a strong man to find the way in.

The circus giant

Giovanni Belzoni was an Italian showman. He was 6 feet 7 inches tall, and powerfully built. In 1815 Belzoni went to Egypt to try to sell a water pump to the ruler. Instead he found himself paid to carry off old Egyptian treasures to the British Museum in London. Belzoni not only forced his way into the pyramid of Khafre. He admitted that he came to rob.

Other early archaeologists were even more ruthless. Colonel Richard Howard-Vyse, a British excavator, used gunpowder to enter the third pyramid, that of Menkure (Mycerinus) in 1837. Vyse and his assistant, John Perring, also investigated the oldest of all the pyramids.

Above: The step pyramid of Zoser at Saqqara near the ruins of Memphis.

Above right: Section of the pyramid of Cheops, or Great Pyramid.

Below: Belzoni's men move the 8-ton stone head of Ramses II across the desert to a Nile river-boat. He built a timber platform. A huge team using ropes dragged it across the sand on rollers.

The so-called Step Pyramid at Saqqara stands 15 miles south of Cairo. This pyramid was built for the Pharaoh Zoser, who reigned about 2600 BC. Before Zoser's time a royal tomb had been no more than a *mastaba* – a flat, rectangular stone or brick structure with the burial chamber deep in the ground below it. Zoser's tomb was a pile of mastabas, stepped one of top of another.

So many early archaeological expeditions were intent on plunder that a great many of Egypt's treasures were shipped to Europe and later America. Such were Cleopatra's Needles, giant stone pillars now in London and New York. It was not until the 1850s that a young Frenchman, Auguste Mariette, founded the Egyptian Antiquities Service. This at last established some control over such finds.

Lifting the Layers

A 19th-century soldier-archaeologist showed how to study the past by lifting one layer of soil at a time.

Until the late 19th century, digging up the past was little more than selfish treasure hunting. The search for valuable statues led men to smash their way through sites. They did not try to understand the ruins they uncovered.

The soldier archaeologist

The careful work of modern archaeology began with one man – the British General Augustus Lane-Fox Pitt-Rivers (1827–1900). Pitt-Rivers was a soldier for much of his life. But he had a keen interest in archaeology. In 1880 he was left a big estate at Cranborne Chase in Dorset. This made him rich enough to spend much time and money on his hobby. Yet instead of heading for the famous ruins of Italy or Egypt, Pitt-Rivers set about exploring the countryside in and around his estates. Wherever he found signs of Iron Age villages or Bronze Age burial mounds he carefully dug trenches. He also made drawings of everything he discovered.

Pitt-Rivers was especially interested in the ordinary objects that litter most ancient sites. These relics, he felt, were a major clue to the everyday lives of the people of the time.

Above: Careful drawings and notes made by General Pitt-Rivers. Above left: At Karnak in Egypt, diggers unearth the store rooms of a temple. Below: Objects unearthed during digs.

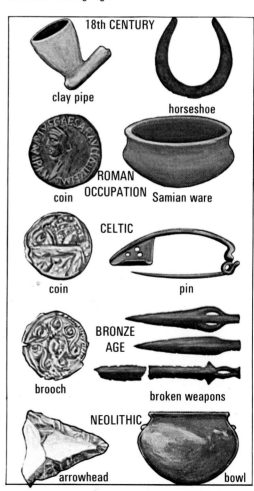

18th CENTURY
clay pipe
horseshoe

ROMAN OCCUPATION
coin
Samian ware

CELTIC
coin
pin

BRONZE AGE
brooch
broken weapons

NEOLITHIC
arrowhead
bowl

As an old soldier, Pitt-Rivers knew that early guns had gradually been replaced by new and often better kinds. This made him think that maybe all of Man's tools, weapons, and ornaments had altered through the ages. He felt that it would therefore be possible to describe objects not only by the region from which they came but also by their likeness to each other.

Stratigraphy

Pitt-Rivers was one of the first archaeologists to study the layers or strata bared by the spade. This study is known as stratigraphy. A place lived in for a long time contains a record, however sketchy, of the life of the people who lived there. This record is to be found in the rubbish that piles up over the centuries until the site becomes a true garbage can of history. When an archaeologist explores a site, he searches the collected layers for clues to how people lived.

One very important rule always holds true for a site that has never been disturbed. The layers at the bottom are older than those above. Once an archaeologist has found the pattern of the layers, he can build up a complete picture of the history of a place.

To do so he digs a trench to cut a slice through as many layers as possible. Each layer can then be identified either by its color or texture or substance.

A trench may reveal a jumble of old building foundations, fragments of walls, packed mud floors, garbage pits, and ash layers where there were once hearths or where fire destroyed a building. These are mixed with soil, rocks, bits of tools, children's toys, broken pottery, and even pieces of jewelry. The layers may be further interrupted where wells, graves, or cellars were dug or where badgers and rabbits have tunneled. Archaeologists must be able to sift through these fragments in order to piece together the clues that reveal the history of the people who once lived on the site.

A trench cut into an ancient European site reveals layers of collected debris. The Bronze Age level contains a "founder's hoard" of broken weaponry gathered to be melted down. Post holes from Celtic times are the remains of a wooden stockade. This was replaced by a stone wall after the Roman conquest. An ash layer reveals that in the battle the site was set on fire.

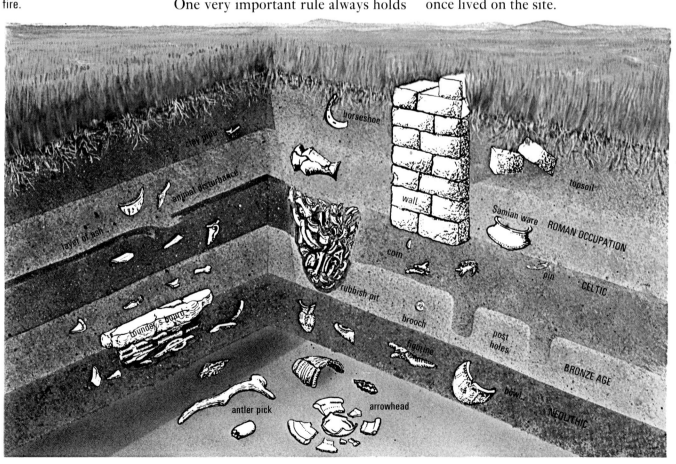

Cities of Homer

The search of a German self-made millionaire proved old tales of Ancient Greece to be true.

Schliemann's wife, Sophia, with the "jewels of Helen" found at Troy. They were lost in World War II.

Schliemann's men dug to the layer he had chosen. They missed Homer's Troy on the way.

In the 19th century most educated people knew the story of the siege of Troy, told by the Greek poet Homer in the *Iliad*. But few believed it to be true. One who did was a small boy, Heinrich Schliemann, son of a poor German priest. Seeing a picture in a book of the attack on the walls of Troy, he said to his father: "Papa, if those walls really existed, they must still be there, buried in the dust. One day, I'll dig them up."

From the age of 14, Schliemann had to earn his own living. He worked hard. In 1846 he set up as an indigo dealer in

Work at Hissarlik has continued since Schliemann's time. The holy well from layer VIII is among the remains that can be seen today.

Russia and soon became immensely rich.

In 1858 – by now a millionaire at 36 – Schliemann gave up business and began to travel. Ten years later, he set out to look for the ruins of Troy.

The tradition

Homer's *Iliad* dates from some time in the 8th century BC. But Schliemann saw it as a true guide to the places that it named. He studied the story carefully to find just where Troy lay. He decided that the likely site was Hissarlik, a mound in northwestern Turkey.

On October 11, 1871, Heinrich Schliemann led his gang of workmen on to the mound for the first of his four digs there.

Directed by Schliemann and his young Greek wife, the diggers worked their way slowly through layer upon layer of ruined material, the remains of many settlements. After a total of 11 months' work, spread over two years, Schliemann told the world that he had at last found the ancient city of Troy.

Schliemann's claim was greeted by the history world with scorn. Discouraged by the scholars' disbelief, he decided to stop digging. On June 14, 1873, the day before he was due to leave, he noticed a copper object in a wall near the building he had named the "Palace of Priam." Behind it, he could see the gleam of gold.

Schliemann knew that thieves and the Turkish government would want to lay their hands on any treasure there might be. Therefore he decided to send his workmen away. Working alone, the Schliemanns uncovered a great treasure of gold, silver, and jewelry.

The city Schliemann had uncovered was indeed Troy, but not the Troy of Homer. The palace and treasure were much older than Homer's story, and belonged to an earlier city on the site, destroyed about 2200 BC. There have been nine settlements or cities on the site, the

HOMER'S EPICS

Homer's long epic poem the *Iliad* describes how a Greek force led by King Agamemnon besieged the city of Ilium (Troy) for ten years to win back Helen, the wife of the Greek King Menelaus. Helen had run away with Paris, son of King Priam of Troy.

The grave circle where Schliemann found the bodies of 19 Mycenaean nobles. Left: A gold ring from Tiryns.

oldest going back to about 3000 BC. The Troy of Homer's story was in layer VII, a small fortified town which perished in flames, with every sign of violence.

The royal graves at Mycenae

Schliemann next turned his attention to Mycenae and Tiryns, in southern Greece. According to Homer, Mycenae had been the birthplace of King Agamemnon, and "Tiryns of the great walls" the home of some of the Greek warriors.

Schliemann explored the fortress of ancient Mycenae. He found five graves, containing the bodies of 19 men, women, and children. Many of the bodies bore gold ornaments – masks, breastplates, headbands, rings, and bracelets. There were other treasures besides.

In the fifth grave were the bodies of three men. All wore golden face-masks and breastplates. As Schliemann raised the masks of the first two, their skulls crumbled away. But the face of the third man was perfectly preserved under its mask. Schliemann was convinced, wrongly, that the remains were those of Agamemnon. They in fact belonged to a time 400 years earlier. But that night, Schliemann sent a triumphant telegram to the King of Greece: "Today I have gazed on the face of Agamemnon."

A gold rhyton in the shape of a lion's head. This jug was used at Mycenae for pouring offerings of wine to the gods.

13

Ur of the Chaldees

In the 1920s Sir Leonard Woolley unearthed the royal Sumerian city of Ur, birthplace of Abraham and one of Mesopotamia's richest cities.

Sir Leonard Woolley liked to say that he was the first to make a living out of archaeology. He studied at Oxford to be a priest and became an archaeologist by accident. It happened when he was sent to Oxford's Ashmolean Museum to work under Sir Arthur Evans, famous discoverer of ancient Crete.

In 1907, at the age of 27, Woolley found himself in charge of digging up a Roman fort in northern England. He had never seen a dig before. But his work was successful. Woolley's priestly training gave him an interest in the Bible lands. He made many visits to Mesopotamia, the "cradle of civilization," before and after World War I. In 1922 he was put in charge of an expedition to dig up the lost city "Ur of the Chaldees."

A gold bull's head decorates a lyre. Several such musical instruments were found in Ur.

The city of Ur

The Bible had kept alive the name of Ur for centuries only as the birthplace of Abraham. Yet for 2500 years this Sumerian capital had been one of the greatest cities of Mesopotamia. In 1854 its site had been found about ten miles from the present course of the Euphrates River, 200 miles from the Persian Gulf. The highest mound on the site hid the Ziggurat, a massive fortress-temple built in several platforms. These great buildings

This figure of a goat with its forefeet in a tree came from the Royal Tombs at Ur.

once rose high above ancient Mesopotamian cities. But before Woolley's expedition, no one had done much to explore them. All around was simply, in Woolly's words, "a waste of unprofitable sand." "It seems incredible," he wrote, "that such a wilderness should ever have been habitable to man, and yet the weathered hillocks at one's feet cover the temples and houses of a very great city."

The royal graves

Woolley began by digging up the great cemetery area: a mass of graves. Many lay one above the other. The older layers dated from 3500 to 3100 BC. They held not only the tombs of citizens, but those of the kings of Ur. Here Woolley found a magnificent gold dagger and a container of tiny gold toilet articles – the first signs

The Royal Standard of Ur shows scenes of Sumerian life done in lapis lazuli, shell, and pink limestone.

of the splendor to come. "Nothing like these," he wrote, "had ever before come from the soil of Mesopotamia."

Many of the tombs had been robbed, but not all. Woolley won lasting fame for his incredible skill in preserving objects on the point of crumbling into dust: these included wigs and gold hair ribbons and a wonderful harp of which only the decorations were intact. And in these royal tombs was waiting the greatest surprise of all. Each royal ruler had the company of neat rows of skeletons – in one tomb there were six men and 68 women. And these were not slaves: they had died richly dressed and wearing splendid jewels. Nor were they unwilling sacrifices, for nowhere was there the slightest sign of violence. Rather, these were the servants of the king – happy to die with him in the hope of being able to go with him to the next world. With them were the skeletons of the oxen that had drawn the funeral sledge to the tomb.

Digging up the Flood

Woolley also excavated a large part of the city where people had actually lived. He unearthed the grand houses of wealthy merchants, a street chapel, and even a school. He decided the city had held more than 250,000 people.

Deep under the layers of human dwellings Woolley came upon a great layer of river clay more than eight feet thick. Now, in the records of the kings of Sumeria there was mention of a flood. Woolley believed it had occurred around 4000 BC, covering a large area of southern Mesopotamia with muddy water. It was the memory of this flood, he realized, that had inspired the Sumerian story of Gilgamesh and the story of Noah and the Flood in the Bible. So, in 1929, came Woolley's telegram to London that was to make headlines all over the world: "We have found the Flood!"

A necklace of lapis lazuli and carnelian beads found at Ur. The people of Ur were skilled metalworkers and jewelers.

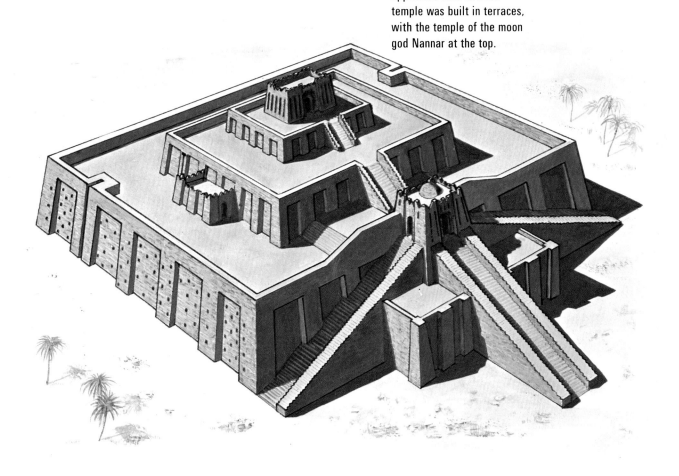

How the Ziggurat at Ur once appeared. This fortress-temple was built in terraces, with the temple of the moon god Nannar at the top.

Warriors of the Sun

Great Indian civilizations flourished for centuries in the jungles and mountains of the Americas. But none long outlasted the arrival of European invaders. Within 50 years fine cities were empty ruins.

One day, John Lloyd Stephens made a chance find in a New York bookstore. He bought an early book about old Indian civilizations of Central America. Stephens was so excited he sailed to Honduras to visit the ruins himself. With him in 1839 went his friend, the British architect and artist Frederick Catherwood.

From the city of Belize, the two men traveled inland. Their first discovery was the ancient Maya ceremonial center of Copán. Here, in a remote valley, Stephens and Catherwood were amazed to find great buildings hidden beneath the jungle. Clambering about in the forest gloom, they saw crumbling walls, terraces and pyramids. While Stephens set about mapping the vast site, Catherwood began sketching the ruins.

Chichén Itzá

The story of their travels thrilled New York. Three years later they returned to explore the Yucatán Peninsula in southern Mexico, the heart of the Maya empire. Here they found many ceremonial centers. Best preserved and most spectacular was Chichén Itzá. It was a sprawling network of courts, plazas, and step pyramids crowned by squat temples. These were covered with carvings of serpents, eagles, jaguars and other beasts. Many held human hearts, a horrible reminder of the living sacrifices that the Maya offered to their gods.

Chichén Itzá was more like a vast monastery than a town. Priests, warriors, and craftsmen had lived there while peasants farmed the surrounding land.

The Maya erected carved stone pillars or ''stelae'' with images of their rulers and hieroglyphs (a writing system based on pictures) giving events and dates.

More than 1200 years before Europeans reached the New World, the Maya Empire flourished in the jungles of Central America. Below, Catherwood's drawing of the temple at Tulum, Mexico.

Like other Maya centers, Chichén Itzá grew fast around AD 500, but was abandoned in the 10th century to the Toltecs from northern Mexico. The city revived in Toltec times, and its finest buildings date from the 11th–13th centuries. Indians finally left Chichén Itzá in the 1400s, perhaps because their water wells dried up.

The mightiest empire

The great Inca civilization of Peru suffered a crushing defeat at the hands of a tiny group of Spanish invaders. In the 1530s Francisco Pizarro, with fewer than 200 soldiers, toppled this great warrior kingdom. Those who were not killed escaped to remote mountain hideouts where they resisted the Spaniards for another 40 years. One hideout, known as Vilcabamba, the Spaniards never found.

Over the next 300 years, the legend of a lost Inca capital continued to survive. The American explorer Hiram Bingham became fascinated with the story of a last outpost of a once mighty empire. In 1911 he set off for Peru to look for it. In the jungle wilderness of the Urubamba River, one of the last unexplored regions of Peru, he discovered a lost town perched high on a narrow ridge next to the peak of Machu Picchu. Bingham toiled up the last few feet of the wall-like slopes with his Indian guides. He reached a cluster of buildings and then a group of

Gold llama, one of the lovely metal objects made by Inca craftsmen.
Left: After the Spanish conquest, isolated Machu Picchu became an Inca refuge.
Below: Central and South America held three great civilizations unknown to the rest of the world.

temples. All were built from enormous hand-hewn blocks of granite, some weighing over ten tons. Wide courtyards, terraces, and houses showed that at least 2000 people had once lived in the town. On all sides, they were protected by cliffs plunging 1500 feet into the gorge below. Only a narrow, steep path, that half a dozen men could hold against an army, connected the town with the outside world. Whether or not the ruins were indeed the lost Vilcabamba, the remains of bodies in a cemetery showed that Machu Picchu had been an Inca town. Here, in complete isolation, the last Incas had survived the Spanish conquest.

Figures from a Mixtec codex (document). The Mixtecs of southwest Mexico were conquered by the Aztecs, just before the Spanish came.
Below: Ceremonial center of Tikal, Guatemala.

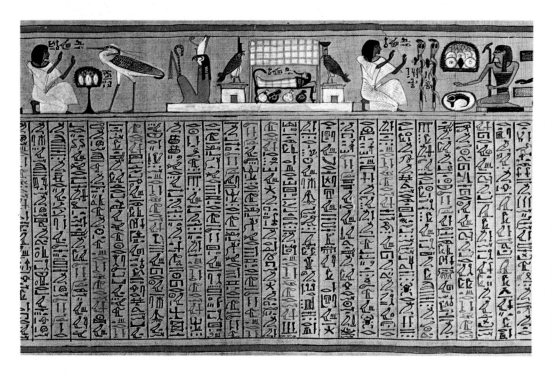

The Papyrus of Hunefar shows Egyptian hieroglyphs. They began as picture writing on clay tablets and papyrus sheets. Eventually, the symbols came to represent sounds.

Below: Champollion deciphered Cleopatra's cartouche by comparing the hieroglyphs with those for Ptolemy, already deciphered. Below, Cleopatra's name in hieroglyphs and letters of the Roman alphabet.

Decoding the Past

K L E O P A T R A

Once men had puzzled out the meaning of old writings, they learned much about the peoples who had used them, long ago.

Left: Egyptian hieroglyphs proved puzzling until men realized that cartouches (oval "boxes") held royal names. The egg in Cleopatra's cartouche shows she was a woman.

Piecing together the past becomes much easier once there is a written record of it. The earliest written languages were long forgotten by the time archaeologists began to take an interest in them. Puzzling out these ancient scripts was a huge problem. But solving it brought great rewards.

Linear B

Arthur Evans spent nearly half a century digging out and restoring ruins of the great Minoan civilization that had flourished on Crete over 3500 years ago. Yet for all his work, Evans was unable to understand the writings on the many clay tablets he unearthed.

Evans went as far as separating three

different scripts. The oldest, in use between 2000 and 1600 BC, was a kind of picture script with tiny stars, arrows, heads, hands, and figures. But so few examples of this script were found that it remains a puzzle to this day. Evans realized the other two scripts used marks that stood for sounds. He named these scripts Linear A and B. Although some 150 tablets of Linear A have turned up on Crete, no one can yet translate it.

Some 4000 tablets of Linear B were found by Evans near the palace at Knossos. The tablets were flat slabs of clay inscribed with a stylus, a sharp, pen-like instrument. When no longer needed, they were thrown away.

Evans did not live to see the decoding

of Linear B. This only took place in 1952, some ten years after his death. The decoder was a young spare-time archaeologist named Michael Ventris. Ventris used methods learned in code-breaking work in World War II. He saw that Linear B had too few kinds of marks to be picture writing and too many to be an alphabet. Thus he guessed the marks must stand for syllables. Using trial and error, by 1953 Ventris had deciphered the tablets.

We now know that the tablets give lists of stores from Knossos. More excitingly, we know the lists are in an early form of Greek.

The Rosetta Stone

During Napoleon's invasion of Egypt, from 1798 to 1801, a French officer noticed a slab of black stone in a fortification that was being pulled down. It had inscriptions in three different scripts. The soldier guessed these were three versions of the same text. The slab ended up in Britain and was named the Rosetta Stone for the place in which it had been found.

The Rosetta Stone provided the key to deciphering ancient Egyptian. It repeated one text in hieroglyphic, the everyday Egyptian demotic script, and Greek.

Below: Cuneiform (wedge shaped) writing was used by the great Mesopotamian civilizations.

A tablet discovered at Pylos in mainland Greece (below) helped men decipher Linear B. Here was proof that the influence of Minoan civilization extended to Greece.

The sites where Linear B tablets were found and the places referred to on the tablets indicate how far Minoan civilization actually spread.

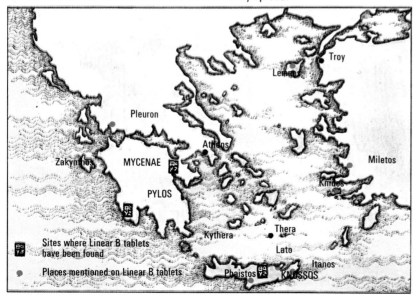

Sites where Linear B tablets have been found

Places mentioned on Linear B tablets

Troy
Lemnos
Pleuron
Athens
Zakynthos
MYCENAE
Miletos
PYLOS
Knidos
Kythera
Thera
Lato
Itanos
Phaistos
KNOSSOS

One of the scripts on it was Greek and the others were two ancient Egyptian scripts.

European scholars had no immediate success in decoding the stone. One person whose imagination was stirred by the Rosetta Stone was a young French schoolboy, Jean-François Champollion. At the age of 18 he had already set to work on a huge history of ancient Egypt and had prepared himself to decipher Egyptian hieroglyphics (a picture script) by learning ancient languages, among them Coptic. Coptic was the final stage of ancient Egyptian that had survived only in the Coptic Church in Egypt.

Champollion knew that the Rosetta Stone's inscriptions were translations of one text, written to mark the crowning of Ptolemy V in 196 BC. An English scholar provided a clue to the hieroglyphs by pointing out the oval "boxes" that seemed to contain certain names. Champollion proceeded by working out the sound equivalents for all the hieroglyphs. But the key to the grammar of the language lay in his knowledge of Coptic. In 1822, 14 years after he began, he finally completed his decoding of ancient Egyptian. His success was a triumph of deciphering, for hieroglyphic bore no relation to any modern alphabet.

Lord Carnarvon (left) and Howard Carter gaze into the Treasury of Tutankhamun. The gilded shrine, protected by four golden goddesses, held internal parts of the king's body. Around were royal belongings. The magnificence of the objects is astounding since Tutankhamun was an unimportant pharaoh who died young.

Valley of the Kings

Digging time had nearly run out for Howard Carter. Then he came upon the treasure-filled tomb of a king of Ancient Egypt.

About a hundred years after sweating workers had dragged huge blocks of stone up earthen ramps to build the Pyramids of Giza, the center of power in Egypt moved much farther south, to Thebes. This royal city lay upon the banks of the Nile where the modern town of Luxor now stands. The Egyptians believed deeply in life after death. Thus they planned their city both for the living and for the dead.

On the west bank of the Nile lies a lonely valley. It is hot, rocky, and sandy, a desolate spot even in the glaring light of the pitiless sun. Into its cliffs workmen tunneled for many years to make graves for the pharaohs – tombs safe from grave robbers. This is the Valley of the Kings, the city of the dead.

The unrobbed tomb

But even in this remote spot the grave robbers were active. They stole many of the treasures buried with the kings. Then, over 3000 years ago, the preserved bodies of about 40 pharaohs were hidden, without treasure, in a shaft to protect

The magnificent death-mask of Tutankhamun, made of gold inlaid with semi-precious stones.

them from thieves. There they remained until 1875, when archaeologists found them by accident. Over the next 40 years scholars discovered most of the royal tombs. But one pharaoh remained a mystery: Tutankhamun. No one knew where he was buried, or his age when he died.

Two British archaeologists made a thorough search for the missing tomb. The fourth Earl of Carnarvon paid for the work. Howard Carter led it. They began in 1914, and worked for eight years, but found nothing. Carnarvon was ready to give up. But in 1922 Carter made a last effort.

Carter thought the tomb might be near that of a later pharaoh, Ramses VI. He cleared away tons of stone chippings thrown out when Ramses's tomb had been dug. His hunch was right: almost at once a stairway leading down into the ground was found. Feverishly, the workers cleared the steps, and came to a door. There in the plaster were the royal seals of the boy king – Tutankhamun.

The glint of gold
Carter stopped work until Lord Carnarvon, who was in England, could join him. Then they opened the sealed doorway and cleared the passage. Thirty feet down they came to another sealed door. Carter pierced a hole through the plaster and held a candle up to look.

"Can you see anything?" asked Carnarvon excitedly.

"Yes – wonderful things!" gasped Carter.

What Carter had seen was, as he later wrote, "strange animals, statues, and gold – everywhere the glint of gold." He was looking into a room 25 feet long, piled to the roof with funeral furniture. At one end of the room was another sealed door. When this was opened, Carter found a gilt shrine which almost filled the burial chamber. It had three more inside it, like a nest of puzzle boxes. Inside the shrines was a stone coffin containing three smaller coffins. The innermost one was made of 300 lb of solid gold. Inside was the mummy (the preserved body) of Tutankhamun.

Most of the treasure is now in the Cairo museum, but the king's body still lies in the tomb. Examination showed that he was a mere lad of 18 when he died. So his tomb had been under preparation for only a short time. Yet in that time more than 1700 items of superb workmanship had been made for it.

Above: A fisherman with a harpoon – a model found among Tutankhamun's treasure.

The front of the Queen's temple of Abu Simbel. On either side of the entrance is a statue of Queen Nefertari flanked by two statues of her husband Ramses II.

Above: This solid gold buckle from Sutton Hoo weighs over a pound. Below: The Sutton Hoo helmet. It is made of iron, covered with bronze plates, and decorated with gold and silver.
Bottom: A buckle and two clips from Sutton Hoo.

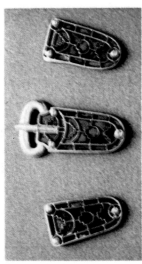

Sea Rovers

Wooden ships buried beneath mounds of earth tell of the ancient seafarers of the north.

In 1938 Mrs E. M. Pretty decided to explore a group of mounds on her property. She was a landowner in the quiet English village of Sutton Hoo, six miles from the Suffolk coast. She hired a local museum worker, who dug into three of the smaller mounds, revealing some Anglo-Saxon remains. The next year he set about opening the largest mound, with the help of Mrs Pretty's gardener.

As the two men dug into the mound, neat lines of iron nails appeared in the earth. And the imprint of the rotted timbers of a boat could still be seen. Archaeologists were called in, and the find was identified as an Anglo-Saxon sea-going ship, 14 feet wide and over 80 feet long, with places for 38 oarsmen. The Viking sea rovers of Scandinavia used to bury dead kings in beached ships with weapons and jewels. Then they had covered the ships with earth. It seemed likely that this was a similar burial.

Indeed in July 1939 the archaeologists suddenly began uncovering jewels and gold coins. Soon there appeared all the magnificently decorated possessions of a warrior king – battle helmet, shield, buckle, and sword. There were more jewels, silver bowls, a small lyre, and a great Byzantine silver dish.

All that was missing was a body. So it was not a burial, but a memorial for a king lost in battle or at sea. Examination of the coins suggested a date of around AD 630. Some historians believe that the man remembered was Roedward, an East Anglian king who died in AD 625.

In 1965 a giant cast of the vessel's imprint in the soil was taken. From this, craftsmen at the British Museum were able to make a full size glass-fiber copy of the boat. The Sutton Hoo treasure, one of the richest ever found in Britain, is also in the British Museum.

Norwegian finds
In 1880 a well preserved Viking longship was unearthed at Gokstad in Norway. It held the skeleton of a man in his fifties – tall and crippled with gout. Another Viking ship was dug from a mound in Oseberg, Norway, in 1903. This beautifully carved state barge held the skeletons of two women. In the ship were the remains of furniture, bedding, tapestries, and other goods for life in the next world. But

Not a trace remained of the timbers of the Sutton Hoo ship, buried in damp English soil. But the iron nails used to rivet its planks were still in position, and sand had formed a complete mold of the ship. A rough cabin in the center held the treasures.

The Gokstad ship is 76½ feet long and 17 feet wide. It was propelled by a square sail and oarsmen. The top of the prow and the stern had decayed.

VIKING VOYAGERS
Between 790 and 1080 Viking ships sailed as far south as the Mediterranean, and in the east Vikings penetrated the heart of Russia. Perhaps the most remarkable voyages of the Vikings were those across the Atlantic to North America. They reached Iceland and Greenland. Then in 1002, old Icelandic tales say that Leif Ericsson landed on a fertile coast where he found wild grapes growing. He called the place *Vinland* (Wineland). Proof of such voyages is a Viking site discovered in Newfoundland in the 1960s.

These Viking glass game pieces were found in Birka in Sweden. But they may have come from Asia. They include a "king" with a crown and are about an inch across.

the mystery remained – who were these magnificent burials for.

The answer was found in the *Heimskringla*, a 13th-century tale of the kings of Norway. It tells of a 9th-century queen, Asa, and her stepson Olaf, who died of gout. We are told, too, that Asa lived to old age, and beneath the place name Oseberg we can see the words "Asa's Berg." So it seems, the Gokstad ship marked the resting place of King Olaf, and the Oseberg ship that of Asa.

The ships of Roskilde Fjord

In 1956 two divers brought up wood from some wrecks in the entrance to Roskilde harbor in Denmark. The timber proved to date from the Viking period. Soon began one of the costliest, most delicate recovery operations ever known. A dam was built around the wrecks and water was pumped out. Gradually the position of every timber was plotted and the fragile wood was removed. Each piece had to be soaked in a tank of warm wax for a year or more. The wax gradually soaked in, replacing parts of the wood that had rotted away under the water. Finally the timbers were reshaped in their original form by being heated until soft, then pressed into a mold.

Using the preserved timbers, the orig-

inal Danish ships were reconstructed. There were five: a light warship, a ferry boat, a small merchantman, a longboat, and a captured deep sea trader. All five had been weighed down with rocks and deliberately sunk about AD 1050. Roskilde, it seems, had been attacked by Norwegian pirates, and this odd assortment of ships had been stripped and sunk to form a sea barrier against the invaders.

The animal-head post from the Oseberg ship. Such heads were carved to frighten enemies.

23

Legend of the Labyrinth

A rhyton or ritual vase in the shape of a bull's head. It is made of soapstone.

New light was thrown on an ancient legend when Arthur Evans dug up a forgotten palace in Crete.

In the trays of an Athenian antique dealer lay some little carved stones. One day an English archaeologist picked them up. Peering short-sightedly at them, he thought he could make out writing of an unknown kind. He asked where the stones had been found. "On the island of Crete," he was told. The archaeologist was Arthur Evans. His excavations on Crete led him to discover a fantastic and long-forgotten civilization.

The path to Knossos
Arthur Evans was the son of a British archaeologist. He spent several years as a journalist in the Balkan peninsula in the east Mediterranean area. He worked on digs in his spare time. In 1884, at the age of 33, he became Keeper of the Ashmolean Museum in Oxford, and rescued it from years of neglect. This post allowed him plenty of time for travel.

Evans first visited Crete in 1894. Earlier work there had shown that some vast building lay buried at the site called Knossos. Evans eventually managed to buy the site and in 1899 he was able to start his excavations.

Almost at once, a great maze of buildings appeared. It was a vast palace, older than Troy, the work of an unknown and long-lived civilization. Then Evans uncovered two large pieces of a wall painting which showed a youth holding a long vase. The loin-cloth and the vase shown in the painting were like ones depicted in some tomb paintings in Egypt. These showed foreigners bearing gifts for the Pharaoh. Archaeologists now realized that the foreigners had been Cretans – and that the island of Crete must have been the first great European sea-trading power.

A piece of fresco showing the lively way Minoan artists painted.

The oldest throne in Europe stands in the palace at Knossos. The walls behind it are decorated with reconstructed frescos.

Minoan civilization

Evans called this great civilization Minoan, for the legendary King Minos of Crete. He used Egyptian objects at Knossos to help date the stages of Minoan civilization. It had begun about 2500 BC and reached a height in 1500 BC. It was that of a secure and comfort-loving people. The great palace at Knossos and others found on Crete had no strong defensive walls. There were excellent bathrooms and drainage systems. Fine wall paintings showed elaborately dressed, gossiping women, and slim, well-groomed men. Pottery was decorated with pictures of plants and octopuses. And there was a great deal of splendid jewelry.

Theseus and the Minotaur

Evans came across many paintings and statues showing bulls. Some showed a charging bull, and a youth somersaulting over its back. Evans remembered the ancient stories of the Minotaur. This legendary monster – half man, half bull – had lived in a maze, or labyrinth, at Knossos. Every ninth year the citizens of Athens were forced to send seven young men and seven girls as food for the Minotaur. Finally Theseus, a young Athenian, found his way into the labyrith and killed the monster.

Knossos has suffered many earthquakes. Earthquakes can sound like an

Above: The north entrance to the palace of Knossos is guarded by columns. The fresco shows a galloping bull. This picture shows how Evans rebuilt parts of the site.

Left: This Minoan brooch shows two bees with a piece of honeycomb. Cretan jewelers were highly skilled.

angry bull. The Minoans may have felt that there was an angry bull-god beneath the earth. Perhaps the bull-leaping athletes were performing a dance to please him. As for the labyrinth, the palace at Knossos was a confusing jumble of rooms, passages and halls. An object shown in many places there was the double-headed axe or *labrys* – so the palace was the place of the labrys or labyrinth.

Evans spent the rest of his life in excavating Knossos. He reconstructed its buildings and pieced together its history up to its sudden destruction – perhaps as the result of the huge explosion of a nearby volcanic island around 1380 BC. It is through his work that we know of the first great European civilization.

Bull-leaping is often depicted in Minoan art. This fresco shows a man across the bull's back. Girls stand at either end.

Jigsaw of History

The past is a puzzle, a mysterious jumble of unsorted clues. Archaeologists must piece them together before the history of mankind can be fully understood.

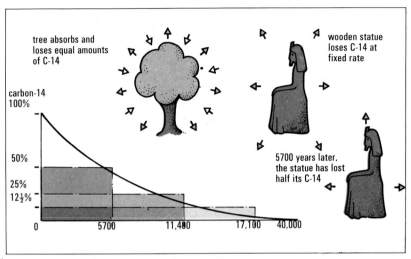

Living things take in radioactive carbon-14. When they die, this decays as the graph above shows. Every 5700 years the amount of carbon-14 in a dead organism drops by half. After 11,400 years then, only a quarter of the original amount remains. A piece of old wood can be dated by comparing its carbon-14 level with that in fresh wood.

A continuous calendar for the US southwest was made by matching overlapping annual rings from successively older trees. It is now possible to date wooden structures in the area dating from AD11 onward.

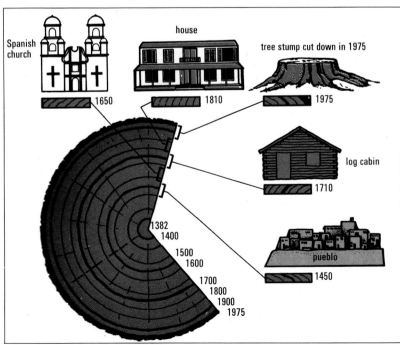

As archaeologists dig up a site, they inevitably disturb and destroy the upper levels. But their job is also to rebuild – to piece together the lives of the people who lived there. This means studying, preserving and restoring the objects that those people left behind.

Dating

How old? is a question archaeologists are always asking of all they find. For knowing the ages of objects can be a valuable guide to the people who used them. The position of an object is often a clue to its date. It can also be dated by comparing it with similar objects of known age. But there are more scientific ways of dating.

The age of a tree can be found by counting its growth rings (you may have seen these on a tree stump). But growth varies from year to year according to the weather. Therefore rings vary in width. Samples from trees of overlapping ages can be used to build up a list of rings going back thousands of years for trees of a certain region.

A valuable means of dating animal and plant remains uses the fact that all living things contain a fixed amount of radioactive carbon-14. When they die this substance decays at a regular rate. By measuring the amount of carbon-14 in an old bit of wood or bone you can find when the plant or animal died.

Reconstructing the past

Digging up a site destroys the protective cover that has preserved objects since ancient times. The first steps of restoration must, therefore, be carried out straight away. Some of the objects unearthed are so fragile that they rapidly break up when exposed to light, air, and moisture. Steps must be taken at once to preserve them in coatings of wax or plastic. Flesh, cloth, and wood generally leave few remains although they sometimes form imprints in the soil. Plaster casts can be made from these, revealing the shape of the original object.

Mosaic pavements too have to be treated on site. (Mosaics are patterns made from colored stones, tiles, or glass set in cement or plaster.) A strong piece of material is glued to the upper surface of the tiles. Then the entire pavement is lifted out of its old bed. The original plaster backing is removed. Broken and missing tiles are replaced, and the entire piece is relaid in a bed of fresh plaster.

Most objects from the site are taken to laboratories for restoration. Fragments of pottery are fitted together and missing bits are replaced with plaster. In the same way plaster is used in putting together skeletons and metal objects.

The 3500-year-old Bull Cup of Cyprus reached the British Museum badly corroded.

X-ray photographs revealed engravings hidden beneath corrosion (above). Cleaning restored the original beauty of the cup (below).

Most metals except for gold decay after thousands of years in the ground. The first step in saving them is to scrape off everything that is not part of the original metal "skin." Then the surface is cleaned and where necessary repaired. A protective coating of resin prevents further decay. X-ray photographs can reveal decorative designs invisible beneath the decay. In a similar way infrared photography can be used to reveal faded patterns on crumbling scraps of cloth.

Past archaeologists have often been criticized for over-restoring objects – filling in missing sections of paintings, for instance. Modern archaeologists prefer to preserve whatever they can save and to alter objects as little as possible.

Some archaeologists have managed to reconstruct whole buildings, using the old materials and methods. But many people think the results seem unlike truly old buildings. Just how much to restore is one problem unlikely ever to be solved.

Above: part of this medieval manuscript was written in carbon black ink. Later some lines were crossed out in iron-gall ink. An infra-red photograph of the same page (below) reveals some of the carbon black script.

Left: a copper-coated mold of the ceremonial helmet of King Mes-Kalem-Du of Ur (2600 BC).

FORGING THE PAST

Early this century, people keenly sought man's early ancestors. In 1908, Charles Dawson found bits of human skull at Piltdown, England. Experts thought the bits 500,000 years old. Much later, tests proved Piltdown Man to have a modern ape's jaw and a human braincase only a few thousand years old.

Archaeological frauds are often carried out for money. Before World War I, the Riccardi family of Italy forged huge statues of ancient Etruscan warriors. New York's Metropolitan Museum of Art bought the statues. The forgery only came to light years later.

Cities in Ashes

The terrible eruption of the volcano Vesuvius buried the town of Pompeii and its inhabitants. But Pompeii was preserved in detail beneath volcanic ash.

About 1900 years ago, Pompeii was a bustling town of some 20,000 inhabitants. It nestled barely a mile from the foot of Mount Vesuvius in southern Italy. For as long as anyone could remember, this volcano had not erupted. Vineyards, olive trees, and pastures clothed its fertile slopes.

Late in August, AD 79, the mountain began to show signs of restlessness. Springs suddenly dried up and tremors rocked the ground. Nevertheless, nobody was prepared for the explosion that shattered the summit on the sultry morning of August 24. In the next few hours, Vesuvius wiped out Pompeii and the nearby town of Herculaneum. Fountains of flame, rock and mud spewed out of the volcano with billowing clouds of ash and steam. A hail of cinders and *lapilli* (small stone fragments) soon began raining on to Pompeii. As the downpour worsened people ran indoors for safety. There some were soon killed by deadly fumes. Others were crushed as the roofs collapsed beneath the rapidly growing layers of stones and ash.

When the eruption died down two days later, Pompeii lay completely buried beneath 12 to 15 feet of stone and ash. At least 2000 people had died in Pompeii. Countless others in the surrounding area had died as they tried to flee to safety. The site of the town itself was abandoned and the memory of Pompeii was soon forgotten.

Rebirth of a city

The rediscovery of Pompeii began by chance nearly 1700 years later. King Charles III of Naples sent an engineer to

Right: Bodies of Pompeiians trapped while fleeing have been recreated by making plaster casts of their imprints in the volcanic ash.
Below: This map shows that Pompeii had been laid out in a regular grid pattern in the fashion of the time. Some 20,000 people lived there.

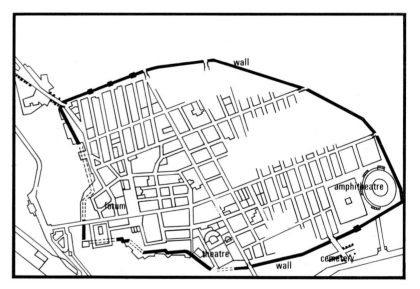

Pompeiian homes were heated by three-legged charcoal-burning stoves.

hunt for marble for a new palace. To the engineer's surprise, the foot of Mount Vesuvius yielded not only a rich supply of marble but also a quantity of beautiful statues. At first the treasures of Herculaneum and Pompeii were recklessly plundered. Digging parties smashed through the ruins in search of frescos, bronzes, and marble statues. The Spanish engineer Alcubierre began the first serious digging at the site in 1748. Then in 1763 an inscription was found that proved the site to be the ancient Roman seaside town of Pompeii.

Excavation shows that the homes of rich Pompeiians had peaceful central courtyards. These let light and air into the houses.

The eruption preserved details of Pompeiian life: eggs and fish on a dining room table, fruit in the market, and loaves in a bakery oven. Beautiful wall mosaics include one warning visitors to "beware of the dog."

The man who brought careful methods of exploration to Pompeii was the great classics scholar, Johann Winckelmann (1717–1768). Winckelmann was chief supervisor for the Roman Catholic Church of antiquities for Rome. He did much to control the reckless looting of the ruins of Pompeii. He also argued that the study of the ancient world was far more than a study of "art for Art's sake." The litter of an ancient civilization was the key to the life of its people. It was a clear guide to the ways in which they had lived, worked, and played. And one way of reconstructing the world of the past was by examining its art. Winckelmann thus proved to be one of the first true archaeologists.

The living dead

Since his time, the excavation of Pompeii has proceeded more or less without a break. In the middle of the 19th century Giuseppe Fiorelli introduced new, careful methods of excavation. He also made plaster casts of the buried dead. When the blanket of ash had

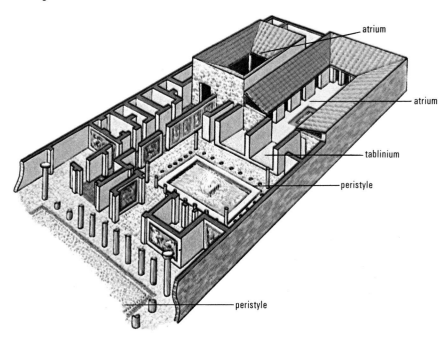

The House of the Faun was an impressive place with its two entrance halls (atrium), two dining rooms, and two gardens (peristyle). Immediately off the atrium was the tablinium – a bedroom, study, and reception room.

settled over Pompeii, it had encased the bodies of its victims. As a body decayed, the exact outline of its shape remained fixed in a hard ashy shell. By forcing liquid plaster into the hollows that remained Fiorelli made likelike casts of these last Pompeiians. The casts were so perfect that they revealed even details of clothing.

The work of excavation at Pompeii still continues. At present, some three-fifths of the town stands revealed. Thanks to the distinguished archaeologist Amedeo Maiuri, finds have been left in place. Thus Pompeii is a museum as well as a monument to the lost splendors of the Roman Empire.

The Past Preserved

Time usually destroys much of the past. But occasionally luck preserves even the delicate remains of living things for thousands of years.

A solid gold bracelet (above) and a gold comb were found in Scythian tombs 2400 years old.

Archaeologists must usually content themselves with studying such long lasting objects as metal and clay tools. From time to time, they have the luck of finding a skillfully preserved body. On very rare occasions they discover human remains that some freak of nature has kept in near perfect condition.

Iron Age murder

In May 1950 two Danish peat diggers hard at work in the Tollund Fen in Central Jutland unearthed the corpse of a man buried eight or nine feet beneath the peat. The body was slightly decayed. But the man's head and dark-complexioned features were well preserved. The diggers immediately reported his murder to the police. The man was indeed found to be a victim of foul play. But he had died nearly 2000 years ago.

It was clear that "Tollund Man" had been deliberately killed. Around his neck was the leather noose with which he had been hanged. Then he had been thrown in a bog. The lower side of his body was especially well preserved for it had long been covered by bog water. Water in bogs and fens is rich in acid. These acids hinder the processes of decay. The iron-rich water also darkens the

A cross-section of a Scythian tomb before robbers broke in and looted it. The scene resembles the inside of a home.

skin to a deep brown color. At the same time the body shrinks slightly in size. Tollund Man may have been the victim of a sacrifice. In Northern Europe during the Iron Age, it was common for human victims to be sacrificed to the goddess of fertility at the beginning of a new year. People thought this ensured the success of the crops in the seasons to come.

Ice tombs

In the late 1920s, a Russian expedition to the Pazyryk Valley near the Mongolian border came across some remarkable graves. They were marked by huge stone heaps. The tombs were burial places of the Scythians, a fierce people who roamed the grasslands of Central Asia during the 9th to 4th centuries BC. Little was known about the Scythians apart from a 5th-century account by the Greek historian Herodotus.

The tombs had been ransacked by tomb robbers. They had not bothered to seal the chambers when they left. Water managed to seep into the open tombs, flooding everything before it froze. The ground in the Pazyryk Valley is not frozen all the year. But the rock piles above the chamber kept out summer warmth. The chambers thus became deep freezers that preserved their contents for the next 2400 years.

The Russian expedition began chipping, then finally thawing its way into the tombs with cauldrons of boiling water. It discovered some of the most remarkable archaeological finds ever.

In Barrow Five, the preserved bodies of two men and a woman were found lying in massive 15-foot coffins carved from tree trunks. The men's bodies were tattooed with elaborate animal designs. On the floor lay a thick Persian carpet and rich hangings covered the walls. Scattered around the chamber were bowls of food, cushions, stools, soft fur-lined clothes, and Chinese silks. Outside the main chamber were buried the chief's favorite riding horses.

Records of the past two centuries tell of more than 150 finds of men, women, and children who were buried in Danish peat bogs. Tollund Man was one of the best preserved corpses ever to be found. The wrinkles on his skin, the light stubble of hair on his chin, and the prints on his fingers have all remained in near perfect condition for over 2000 years.

The Scythians' belief in an afterlife was clear from the way they furnished their tombs like homes. Yet most surprising was the way the tombs fitted Herodotus's descriptions. He wrote: "In the open space around the body of the king they bury one of his concubines, and also his cup-bearer, his cook, his groom, his lackey, his messenger, some of his horses. . . . After this they set to work and raise a vast mound above the grave."

In China, a tomb dating from the 1st century BC held the corpse of a woman. The dry, airless grave had kept her body tissues well preserved.

Cities of the Indus

In the 1940s excavations revealed the remains of a long-forgotten civilization in northern India – two fortified cities carefully laid out in a pattern that would be the envy of any modern town planner.

It was the middle of World War II. A tall, keen-eyed brigadier was strolling back to his tent outside Algiers in the evening sun. But his commanding officer, General Brian Horrocks, waylaid him, waving a signal from London. "I say, have you seen this?" he said. "They want you as Director-General of Archaeology in India. Why, you must be rather a king-pin at this sort of thing! I thought you were a regular soldier."

The brigadier was indeed a king-pin at "that sort of thing." He was Dr Mortimer Wheeler (later Sir Mortimer Wheeler), one of Britain's leading archaeologists.

Archaeology in India

The Indian government, then still under British control, had asked for Mortimer Wheeler. He was needed to teach the Indian Archaeological Survey modern methods.

The most important archaeological sites in the subcontinent of India lie in the Indus valley. They are the ruins of one of the oldest of all civilizations. Today these ruins are in Pakistan.

The ruins were discovered by accident in 1856. Two brothers, John and William Brunton, were in charge of laying a railroad from Karachi to Lahore. John was laying the southern part of the track. He needed stone for the embankments and found it in the ruined medieval town of Braminabad. William also found an old ruined town, near the village of Harappa. There were plenty of bricks there to make firm foundations for his section of the line. What he did not realize was that the bricks were 3500 years old.

Exploration of the Indus Valley had to wait until 1920. Then digs were begun at Harappa and at another city 400 miles to the southwest, Mohenjo-Daro. Many interesting finds were made but nobody was quite sure how old the cities were. It was clear that the inhabitants had used both bronze and stone tools.

Underwater mystery

Wheeler, the archaeologist-soldier, had his first glimpse of Harappa on a May morning in 1944. Its main feature was a huge mound surrounded by piles of yellow mud. Within minutes he had identified the piles of mud. They were the remains of great brick walls which had once formed defenses surrounding the ancient city. Excitedly, Wheeler hurried downstream to Mohenjo-Daro. There he found precisely the same features.

Top: A brick drain in Mohenjo-Daro. Drainage here was excellent. Some houses even had privies connected to the main sewers. Above: Delicately carved Indus seals with animal designs. Below: A pottery fragment from Harappa, a city similar to Mohenjo-Daro.

Wheeler pioneered a new method of excavation in the Indus Valley. Instead of digging trenches, workers dug squares separated from one another by strips of undug earth. This method divides a dig into clear areas and makes all parts easy to get at.

Teams working under Wheeler discovered that most of Mohenjo-Daro had been made of baked brick. From this he guessed the reason why the Indus Valley around the ancient city is now so bare of trees. Wheeler believed that the inhabitants 4000 years ago felled most of the trees for fuel for their brick kilns.

One of the problems for archaeologists at Mohenjo-Daro is that the foundations and thus the oldest part of the city lie underwater. Yearly spring flooding of the Indus over 4000 years has raised the soil water to cover the lowest layer of ruins. Wheeler found water 16 feet down. Helped by pumping and baling he dug down another 10 feet. Then rising water flooded the hole.

But other work on the site revealed a great deal about the city. On a 50-foot man-made mound lay the ruins of a large State Granary, pillared halls, and a Great Bath. Below the mound stretched the town, laid out in a grid pattern with an

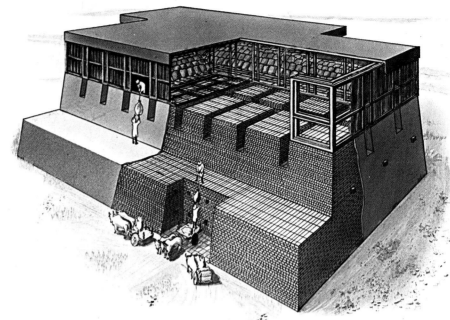

elaborate system of brick drains. A similar plan has been found at Harappa. But so much damage was done by the railroad engineers of the last century that only a general outline of the fortress mound has been recovered. Skeletons of men, women and children, seemingly killed in an attack on Mohenjo-Daro, were found in the upper layers of the ruins. This battle occurred somewhere around 1500 BC. Such attacks on walled cities are mentioned in the *Rig Veda,* the oldest of the sacred books of the Hindu religion. But experts now think that flooding forced the last citizens to leave.

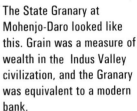

The State Granary at Mohenjo-Daro looked like this. Grain was a measure of wealth in the Indus Valley civilization, and the Granary was equivalent to a modern bank.

This dignified head is one of the few surviving examples of Indus stone sculpture. It may represent a god or priest-king.

The Great Bath at Mohenjo-Daro. Around it are verandahs and smaller rooms with private baths. Priests may have used these.

The Camera's Eye

Science helps the archaeologist to find ancient sites hidden from the human eye. Special tools even show whether a site is worth excavating.

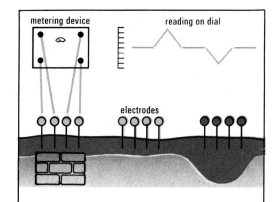

The camera has an important part to play in archaeology in recording finds and photographing sites. But it is also valuable in other ways. Pictures taken from the air and inside unexcavated tombs show objects invisible to people on the ground.

Bird's-eye view

In the 19th century, many archaeologists realized that signs of old fields and burial mounds showed up most clearly from a height. Some even studied the ground from balloons. The development of the camera and of aircraft meant that they could make a lasting record of what they saw, and study this at leisure. One of the first to realize the possibilities was Osbert Crawford, archaeological officer for the British Ordnance Survey just after World War I. One day he was asked to look at strange markings in photographs taken by air force planes. "What I saw far surpassed my wildest dreams . . . ," he wrote later. "Here on these photographs was revealed the accurate plan of field systems . . . at least 2000 years old."

Aerial photographs may reveal a clear pattern in a seeming jumble of, say, mounds and banks. But such photographs may also show up a great deal that cannot be seen from the ground.

RESISTANCE MEASUREMENT

Water is a good conductor of electricity. Soil in filled pits or ditches holds more moisture than undisturbed soil. An electric current passed through moist soil meets less resistance than one passed through dry soil. But soil over old buried paths or walls is drier and more resistant than ordinary soil.

Archaeologists measure soil resistance by a row of electrodes connected to a metering device. These are then moved and more measurements taken. Such measurements reveal buried structures.

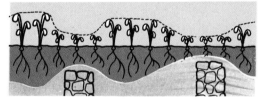

Above: Plants grow better in deep, moist soil than in dry. Soil over the remains of old buildings is often shallower and drier than normal. These differences show from the air.

Below: When the Sun is low, even slight bumps and dips in the soil cast shadows. Aerial photographs of such shadows on plowed land or pasture may show traces of old buildings.

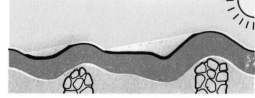

An infrared aerial photograph of crop marks shows ancient structures. Circles are Bronze Age burials, rectangles are Iron Age fields.

Shadow, soil, and vegetation marks

Photographs taken at a low angle when the Sun is near the horizon reveal shadows thrown by very small bumps and dips in the ground, and can show a pattern of long-forgotten ditches and banks. For land which has once been disturbed is never quite the same again, no matter how many times it has been plowed over.

Disturbed soil is also usually slightly different in color from undisturbed soil. Filled-up ditches and holes leave moist pockets of earth rich in humus. Crops flourish here. But hidden walls thinly covered with soil show as lines of stunted growth. All this can be clearly seen from the air. From on high, areas of strong and weak growth show up as patterns made up of differing tones of green.

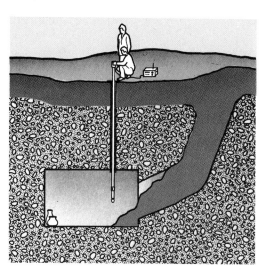

A camera and flashlight are lowered through a hole drilled in a tomb. Photographs reveal the contents and show if excavation is worthwhile.

Probing the tombs

Aerial archaeology has played a very important part in excavations of Etruscan tombs. The Etruscans ruled over central Italy before the Romans. Because their civilization was ruthlessly destroyed by the Romans little is known about them.

The Etruscans buried their dead in cemeteries outside their cities, with *tumuli* or mounds raised over the tombs. These tumuli have long been leveled, but the fragments of building material that remain leave lighter circles clearly visible in aerial photographs.

Many thousands of Etruscan tombs have now been found. It would take more than a lifetime to dig up all of them. Many are anyway empty. Thus, which ones are worth opening? To solve this problem the camera is again brought in. First, a small hole is drilled down through the roof of the tomb. Then the archaeologist lowers a probe with a tiny camera and a flash light. As the probe is turned around, the camera takes a series of pictures. These show the inside of the tomb. Archaeologists can then decide if it is worth excavating.

A magnificently carved Etruscan urn.

Etruscans decorated their tombs with paintings of scenes from daily life. This painting shows a procession in honor of the goddess Ceres.

35

Princes of Jade

In 1973 the Western world saw an exciting exhibition of old Chinese art. All the pieces had been found since World War II, by workers as well as archaeologists.

This leopard, of gilded bronze with garnet eyes, is one of four found in the tomb of Tou Wan. They are about 1½ inches in height.

Twin cups made of gilded bronze inlaid with jade. The bird is a phoenix. In its beak it holds a jade ring.

China has the oldest unbroken civilization in the world. But archaeology only began in China this century. This is partly because most Chinese once worshiped their ancestors and felt it wrong to disturb their graves.

Modern excavations

The first digs in China were made in the 1920s with great success. Remains were found of Peking Man, who lived 500,000 years ago. Also the Bronze Age Shang capital of An-yang was excavated. But during the 1930s the Japanese invaded China and archaeological work came to an abrupt halt. In 1949 Communist China came into being. Since then the

Above: Workers break down the brick wall guarding the tomb of Liu Sheng. Below: Sorting out the objects found in Liu Sheng's tomb.

Chinese have opened many sites. Most exciting of all were perhaps the royal tombs of Liu Sheng of the Han dynasty and his wife Tou Wan. Both died late in the 2nd century BC.

A prince's tomb

In June 1968 some soldiers stationed on a mountain in north-east China found bricks set into a limestone cliff. The soldiers reported their find and soon archaeologists arrived. The bricks were removed, revealing a man-made tunnel leading deep into the rock.

Making their way past fallen rocks and rubble, the archaeologists at last reached a vast underground room, it was some 50 feet by 40 feet, and more than 25 feet high. On the floor stood a neat array of bronze and pottery vessels, figures carved from stone, and the remains of chariots. At the far end was a door of massive stone slabs. It had been sealed with molten iron. Beyond was a chamber full of what seemed to be heaps of dust. But beneath the grime were beautiful objects of bronze and jade, gold, silver, and pottery. There were also scraps of lacquered wood – all that remained of a magnificent coffin. Amid these pieces lay jade tablets. These had once been wired together with gold to form a burial suit for a man.

Tell-tale chippings of rock not far away from the tomb entrance led to the discovery of a second tomb. This was very like the first, but it held the body of a woman. She too wore a suit of jade and was surrounded with precious objects.

Archaeologists worked out that it must have taken huge teams of men many months, if not years, to hollow out these tombs. They also figured it would take a craftsman ten years to make one jade suit. Clearly these were the tombs of very important people. This was proved by inscriptions on bronze pots. These named

the man as Liu Sheng, King of Ching-shan and son of the Emperor Ching. The woman had been Liu Sheng's wife Tou Wan who died some ten years later. Liu Sheng was known for his love of luxury and good living. This and the custom of surrounding a dead noble with goods he might need in the afterlife accounts for the splendor of the objects around him.

A gilded bronze lamp partly shaped as a kneeling servant. Sliding openings control the amount and direction of the light. The smoke rises through her right sleeve and into her body. The lamp was found in the tomb of Tou Wan.

This bronze horse also dates from the Han dynasty; it was found in 1969 in a tomb in north China. This type of horse was prized by warriors for its speed and size and for its hard hooves. The statue is 13½ inches high.

THE BURIAL SUITS

Jade, a hard green stone, was greatly valued by the Chinese. To them it stood for purity and virtue. Liu Sheng's suit was made of 2690 separate pieces. Each piece had been carefully shaped and polished, pierced at each corner, and linked with those next to it by knots of heavy gold thread. So skillfully had the pieces been worked that they formed a close-fitting suit. It even had a special nose compartment.

Tou Wan's suit was smaller, and the jade around the upper part of her body was joined by silk binding to a backing of silk. The jade of both suits was originally a beautiful light green. But age has given it a milky look.

The funeral suit of Tou Wan. Around it are jade disks. These are symbols of heaven.

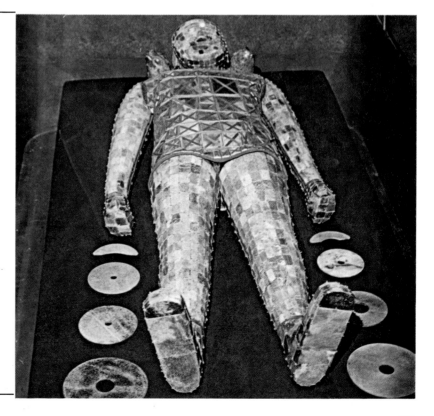

Measuring a cannon found on a wreck.

Underwater Discoveries

Sunken wrecks fascinate everyone. Excavating them sets unusual problems for the archaeologist.

Underwater archaeology is the study of old objects found under water. These include wrecks and ruins in the sea, in rivers and in lakes.

Water preserves some materials, including wood and fabrics, which would very soon rot away if exposed. On the 17th-century Swedish warship *Vasa*, for example, the bodies of sailors were found with their clothes still perfectly preserved.

But underwater archaeology also has its disadvantages. By far the greatest of these is simply the difficulty in working under water. The first modern divers were hampered by heavy helmets and bulky suits. Instead of diving, men could drag the water with nets or grappling irons. But these often destroyed what archaeologists were trying to save. It is only in the last 30 years that the develop-

ment of the aqualung has set the underwater archaeologist free.

Working under water

Underwater sites can be found in a number of different ways. Written records may give details of wrecks – their cargoes and why and where they sank. But a wreck is seldom easy to find. The chance discovery of coins, cannon, or other objects often provides a clue to the wreck they came from. Even strange formations of coral can indicate a wreck to the diver with a practiced eye. The ancient ship-

Gun-carriages on the Vasa's lower gun-deck. Like other iron objects, the guns needed treatment to stop them crumbling.

THE "VASA"
One of the most famous underwater finds was the Swedish warship *Vasa*. She had been launched in 1627, and sank in Stockholm harbor on her maiden voyage. In 1956, a Swede, Anders Framzen, found the vessel after years of searching with wire drags and grapnels. In 1961 the warship was raised by steel cables attached to floats. She now stands in a Stockholm museum. Special treatments were needed in order to preserve the fragile iron and woodwork.

ping routes of the Mediterranean, Baltic, and Caribbean are likely sites of wrecks, especially near danger points such as reefs or submerged rocks.

When the general area of a wreck has been located, divers search it piece by

This bronze jockey on horseback dates from the 2nd century AD. It was found in the sea near Athens. The horse needed heavy restoration.

This shish-kebab, found off the Turkish coast, came from the galley of a ship of about 1200 BC. Small pieces of meat were threaded on the skewers and grilled.

piece so that they cover every foot of sea floor in the area. If they are lucky enough to find and identify the wreck, then the area containing it is marked off, often in the sort of grid pattern used on land. Much of the underwater archaeologist's work is very like that of the archaeologist on land. But the rules of careful excavation, detailed recording, and labeling are harder to keep. For under water, shifting sand, currents, and tides can often change a site overnight.

Hidden dangers

Excavation under the sea is dangerous work. The diving team must be thoroughly familiar with the sea floor and ocean currents and temperatures on the site. Divers take turns to work. Each diver works from 12 to 40 minutes at a time, depending on the depth. He may have to spend several hours in a special chamber before resurfacing to prevent an attack of the "bends" – severe pain or even death caused by nitrogen gas bubbles forming in the bloodstream.

One of the most valuable tools for underwater excavation is the airlift. This clears sand and mud from the site. The airlift consists of a long tube reaching from the surface to the sea floor. High-pressure air is pumped into the bottom of the tube. Sand, mud, and small objects are drawn up the tube with great force.

Some of the equipment used in investigating a wreck.
1 Area grid. 2 Metal detector.
3 Balloon for raising finds.
4 Airlift. 5 Basket for fragile finds. 6 Telephone booth.
7 Camera, fixed above locating grid. 8 Writing on a specially coated board. The hull of the surface ship can be seen at the top.

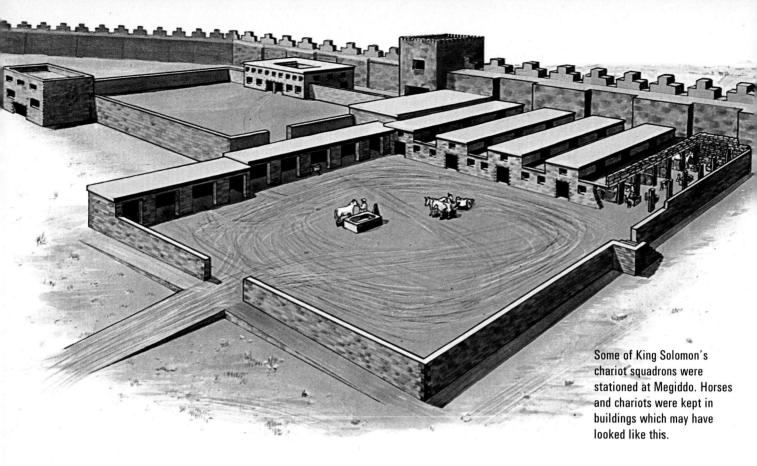

Some of King Solomon's chariot squadrons were stationed at Megiddo. Horses and chariots were kept in buildings which may have looked like this.

From Dan to Beersheba

Old Bible stories have helped archaeologists to find the lost cities of the Holy Land.

"For the king said to Joab the captain of the host, which was with him, Go now through all the tribes of Israel, from Dan even to Beer-sheba, and number ye the people." So wrote the author of the Second Book of Samuel, long ago. Even today much of Israel lies between Dan in the north, and Beersheba on the edge of the Negev Desert.

Israel and west Jordan make up most of Palestine – an area famous in Bible stories. Few other regions have such a ready-made guide to archaeological sites as the Bible. For much of the Bible is old Jewish history, and archaeologists have proved it right time after time.

From pilgrims to scholars

The earliest archaeological reports on Palestine came from pilgrims, men such as the Dominican friar Felix Schmid in the 1480s, or the English clergyman Henry Maundrell in the early 1700s.

But the first real studies came in the 1800s. In a three-month exploratory trip in 1838 two Americans, Edward Robinson and Eli Smith, identified the sites of many dozens of biblical cities. This more than doubled what was already known about Palestine. In 1865 the British established the Palestine Exploration Fund. This paid for a series of expeditions to sites in the Holy Land. But none of the archaeologists working over the sites could date what he found with any precision – until the arrival on the scene of Flinders Petrie in 1890.

Petrie was a remarkable man. He was sent to Egypt by his father to measure the Pyramids to support strange religious notions. He failed to prove the theories but made the most careful survey of the Pyramids ever carried out.

An ostrakon thought to have been used in the final drawing of lots at Masada. The Hebrew letters spell Ya'ir – the name of the Zealot commander.

Armed with the knowledge he had gathered from his earlier work, Petrie investigated Tel el-Hesi in southern Palestine. *Tel* is an Arabic word meaning "hill," and many tels are actually the ruins of ancient towns. Petrie found distinctive pottery at every level in the tel. He was able to date some of the pottery because it was like some of the Egyptian ware he had already discovered.

The dry desert climate at Masada preserved things like this sandal and basket that would normally rot away. Other items included scroll fragments of biblical texts.

The great rock of Masada was the scene of the Jews' last stand against the Romans in AD 73. Camps built by the attacking Romans still lie below the hill.

Digging up the Bible

Since Petrie's time dozens of expeditions have dug up parts of Palestine. In 1903 a German expedition discovered at Tel el-Mutesellim, six miles south-west of Nazareth, the remains of Megiddo. This ancient walled city had flourished at the time of Solomon, the greatest king of Israel. An even more thorough search was undertaken by an American team, directed by Clarence Fisher, Gordon Loud and P. L. O. Guy. The dig began in 1925, and continued until 1939. As they sliced their way through the mound, the team found inscriptions and remains of Babylonian and Assyrian occupation. But in a deeper layer they came across a large paved area, studded with the remains of stone pillars. They had stumbled across a huge stable block, big enough to hold more than 450 horses. From biblical references they believed that Megiddo was one of the royal stables of Solomon, who had 1400 chariots.

One of the most exciting excavations was undertaken in the 1960s by an Israeli team led by Professor Yigael Yadin, and helped by volunteers from other lands. The site was Masada, a rock fortress near the Dead Sea. Here a group of religious Jews called Zealots made their last stand against the Romans in AD 73. Yadin's team found evidence not only of the siege but also of its gruesome ending. In a small cave in the side of the southern cliff were scattered the bones and skulls of about 25 people. They alone were left of the defenders of Masada, who had killed themselves rather than surrender to the Romans. Ten of the Jews were chosen by lot to execute the rest, and then drew lots among themselves to decide which of them should finish the slaughter and then kill himself. And among the finds were 11 *ostraka*, inscribed pieces of pottery. Each bore a name. It seems these were the very ostraka used for casting lots on that last, fatal day.

On Site

Amateurs and professionals work with the greatest care to uncover the secrets of the past.

"There is no right way of digging, but there are many wrong ways." So wrote Sir Mortimer Wheeler, one of the greatest 20th-century archaeologists. When digging up the past, there is always a risk of destroying valuable evidence. But good archaeologists work methodically, and note everything they find before it is disturbed.

The diggers

The leader of an archaeological dig must have great experience and learning. He also needs much the same skills of leadership and organization as an army officer. Indeed some of the most successful archaeologists were once soldiers.

The director usually has a staff of about a dozen skilled people, and a much larger number of actual workers. On anything but a small dig, the director has a skilled and experienced deputy. On a large dig more than one area may be excavated at the same time. Here there is a supervisor for each area. An experienced foreman handles the heavy digging.

Removing earth and finding objects is only part of the work. Specialists must record everything that is found and its exact position. A draftsman makes accurate on-the-spot drawings and plans. A surveyor surveys and maps the site before and during excavation.

Many objects are in a very fragile or decayed condition when they are discovered. Thus a chemist must be on hand to preserve the finds until they can be given treatment in a laboratory. Another specialist is the small-finds recorder, who keeps careful records of all the finds,

photographer on gantry

washing pottery

pottery grid

cleans them, and labels them. He is backed up by an expert on pottery. Pottery is one of the greatest aids to dating archaeological finds. Someone who can date bits of pottery, or *shards*, can help the dig enormously. Identifying coins is also a great help.

Finally, there are the laborers. Some may be hired: building workers have the right sort of experience for much of the heavy earth-shifting. Most large digs rely heavily on volunteers to do the lighter and more detailed work. Many are university students on vacation.

The site

Most sites are chosen for excavation because of clues to what lies buried. In open country aerial surveys are a great help. Many old sites – particularly Roman ones – have rather similar layouts. A knowledge of what is likely to be there makes it easier to recognize what is actually found.

Digging under cover. The plastic tent stops rain ruining the carefully cleared surface.

surveying

grid marked out with pegs

site plan

drawing a section

scale rod

tape measure

spirit level

knives

g and recording finds

Above: The grid system of excavation. It is a great help in the orderly running of a large dig.

Below: These skeletons were labeled and a scale provided so that the photograph is a permanent record.

The director begins by marking off the site with his surveyor. Then he selects the areas where the actual digging will take place. Sometimes it is necessary to explore a site by cutting a trial trench across it. But the best way of digging is to take a square of ground and go methodically downwards within the limits of the square. If the site is large enough a series of squares can be dug out, forming a grid pattern with earth walls between.

Digging begins with spades and picks. But when undisturbed levels are reached more delicate, precise tools are needed. Small plastering trowels and old table knives make good tools for gently scraping away the soil around an object. Small, soft paint brushes are used to remove the final traces of soil. Then the object can be sketched or photographed before it is removed. Workers have labeled trays and baskets beside them. Into these they put the finds for labeling and recording.

General Pitt-Rivers said that "a discovery dates only from the time of the record of it, and not the time of its being found in the soil." Until other archaeologists can read about it, a dig has no scientific value. A really detailed record overcomes the great snag of archaeology – the destruction of evidence.

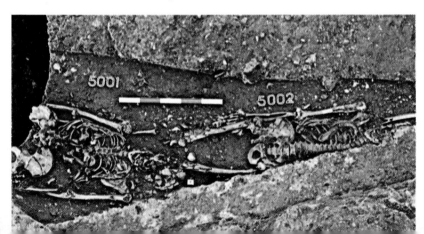

5001

5002

Chance Discoveries

Not all archaeological discoveries result from a deliberate search. Evidence of the past is often uncovered by accident.

The Battersea shield – a bronze shield of the 1st century BC. It was dredged up from the River Thames in London.

The archaeologist digs into the earth in search of the past. But occasionally someone or something else disturbs the earth, and the past is unexpectedly revealed. A storm can expose a buried wall. A shower of rain wash mud from a pottery fragment. The pounding of the sea may reveal relics in the faces of cliffs. Sometimes even a day's bad weather will show up what has been overlooked – flints, pottery, small works of art – on sites already under excavation.

Stumbling on the past

The list of human activities that have resulted in chance finds is endless. Greek fishermen have dragged up ancient statues in their nets. Italian coal miners have dug skeletons out of rock. Farmers in the

Volunteers work fast to record a site uncovered by demolition. Soon, deep foundations laid for a new building will destroy the site for ever.

The colorful Stone Age cave paintings at Lascaux in France. Schoolboys found them by chance.

Middle East have struck the buried walls of Roman villas with their plows; and building workers and farm workers all over Europe have chanced upon gold and silver coins, bronze statues, and jewelry. Even war has brought its share of finds in trenches and in bomb craters. And in the last 30 years endless discoveries have been made in the wake of bulldozers.

Not all finds are immediately recognized. On the Isle of Anglesey off north Wales, the chains a tractor driver was using to tow a truck out of the mud proved to be slave chains 2000 years old.

The Caves at Lascaux

Sometimes an archaeological discovery is made simply because no one in modern times has been that way before. Most of these finds belong to the story of exploration rather than archaeology – the finding of lost cities, for example, in Africa and South-east Asia. But one of the greatest archaeological chance finds happened in France – and it was made by a schoolboy.

On a September day in 1940 in the Dordogne region of France, a group of schoolchildren were out hunting rabbits. Suddenly the dog – "Robot" – vanished down a hole in the hillside where a tree had been uprooted in a storm. One of the boys scrambled after Robot and found himself in an underground cave. Around him on the walls were colorful paintings of oxen, stags, horses, and bison. The

THE DEAD SEA SCROLLS

In the Spring of 1947 a young Bedouin shepherd was seeking a stray sheep near the Dead Sea. High up in a rock face he spied a small opening. With two companions he climbed the cliff. They found a cave littered with clay jars containing battered scrolls of leather and papyrus. This dusty den was an archaeological treasure house, for the scrolls proved to be biblical texts from the time of Christ. This and later Dead Sea discoveries have added much to our knowledge of the Bible.

children had discovered the cave of Lascaux – one of the richest painted caves of the Old Stone Age. Its works of art are 20,000 years old.

A Roman palace

In 1960 the driver of a trench digger was at work on a water-main north of the village of Fishbourne in Sussex, England. Suddenly he found he was cutting through a mass of Roman tiles and rubble. News of the find was passed to the local archaeological society. An exploratory excavation was organized. This soon became a full-scale dig when it was learned that the land might be sold for building. The archaeologists hoped to uncover as much as they could. But they also wanted to find enough to arouse public interest in preserving the site. Fortunately by 1962 the Sussex Archaeological Trust had bought the land, and work continued until 1967. What was revealed was the largest Roman palace in Britain. It covered six acres. This massive villa had courtyards, fountains, and mosaic floors. Part of it even had underfloor central heating. The palace dated from a very early period of Roman occupation. It had been a gift to a British king, Tiberius Claudius Cogidubnus, in the 1st century AD.

Each time the earth is disturbed, for new buildings or just a vegetable patch, new finds are likely to appear. This gives the archaeologist almost endless chances for discovery. And each new discovery adds something to our knowledge of the past.

The keen eye of a man digging a water-main led to the discovery of the great Roman palace at Fishbourne, England. Here a mosaic of Medusa is uncovered on the floor of one room.

Mysteries in Stone

Archaeologists can solve mysteries that have puzzled men for hundreds of years. But some problems may never be solved.

Some people saw megaliths as strange shrines – possibly the idea behind this old print of Stonehenge (below). To other people megaliths were just quarries. Carnac (bottom) has lost 2000 stones since 1800.

Perhaps the first monuments to arouse curiosity were the megaliths of Western Europe. These structures, made of huge slabs of rock, are found from Spain to Scandinavia. Most common are barrows – tombs where a rock chamber was covered with earth to form a mound. Even more striking are the "standing stones" of Carnac in Northern France, and Stonehenge in Southern England.

Carnac has huge upright stones in great avenues stretching for hundreds of yards. The highest stones tower upward 21 feet. Archaeologists believe them to be the remains of a great religious center – the scene of solemn processions and sacred ritual.

Stonehenge is a series of stone circles. Its largest megaliths stand some 30 feet high. The monument was built in three phases between 2600 and 1400 BC. It was begun in Neolithic times and finished in Bronze Age times. It may have been both a temple and an observatory. The position of the stones can be used to work out important dates like midsummer. Such dates would have been very useful to a farming people. But archaeologists and historians still argue about how the people who built it used Stonehenge.

Easter Island

Also called megaliths, but very different, are the sculptures of Easter Island. This is a lonely volcanic island in the Pacific Ocean. Its massive stone figures have enormous heads. Some rise 66 feet high. They were made to stand on huge platforms called *ahus*. But the only ones still standing today are unfinished, set up near the quarry from which the stone came. They are signs of a rich culture, with a complex religion and even writing. Very little is known of it now.

The tragedy of Easter Island is that its culture should ever have become a mystery. Discovered in 1722, the island was occasionally visited by European ships. In those days it had a population of several thousand, and its religion was flourishing. But in 1862 1000 islanders were carried off in a Peruvian slave-raid. The handful who survived to return to the island brought smallpox with them. The population quickly fell to a few hundred. Among the dead were nearly all the priests and nobles. With them perished all the old ways of Easter Island, and the secret of their writings.

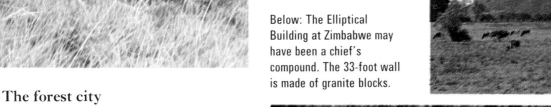

Left: One of the many big statues on Easter Island. Islanders say they represent the Long-Ears – a people who were all killed a long time ago.

Below right: Silbury Hill, Wiltshire, England, is the largest prehistoric mound in Europe. Its purpose is doubtful. Excavations have failed to find the hoped-for rich burial inside.

Below: The Elliptical Building at Zimbabwe may have been a chief's compound. The 33-foot wall is made of granite blocks.

hardly anyone thought that such impressive ruins could be the work of Africans – a people who dwelt in mud huts.

The first careful excavations of Zimbabwe were led by David Randall-McIver in 1905 and Gertrude Caton-Thompson in 1929. They revealed that the ruins were certainly African, because most of the objects found were typical of Africa and nowhere else. Other finds included Arab, Persian, Indian, and Chinese "trade goods" – articles made to be exchanged for gold or ivory. These were proofs that Zimbabwe had traded with far away peoples. The trade goods were also a means of dating. By comparing them with similar objects found elsewhere, archaeologists could tell that Zimbabwe was built in the 9th century AD, and abandoned in the 19th century.

The forest city

In the 1870s reports reached Europe of huge stone buildings, long ruined in the forests of Rhodesia. Some people thought them the biblical source of King Solomon's gold. The site was invaded by a stream of explorers, treasure hunters, and archaeologists, all with different goals.

Different experts had various ideas for explaining Zimbabwe, as the ruins were called. Certain people suggested that it was the land of Punt, where Queen Hatshepsut of Egypt sent an expedition in about 1500 BC. A more likely notion was that Arab settlers had built the city – the Arabs had certainly explored much of Africa, and some of their pottery had been found on the site. But at the time

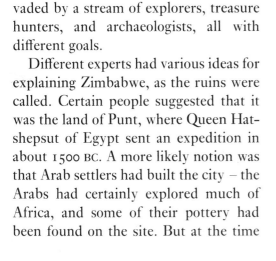

Index

Bold figures indicate major mention
Italic figures indicate illustration or map

Acknowledgments
Photographs: Page 1 Michael Holford; 2 London Museum (top), Sonia Halliday (center), Peter Scoones: Seaphot (bottom); 3 Heraklion Museum, Greece (top), National Museum, Copenhagen (bottom); 4 Sonia Halliday; 5 J. L. Courtney; 6 Michael Holford/British Museum (top), Mansell Collection (center), Thames & Hudson (bottom); 7 British Museum (top & Bottom), Mansell Collection (center); 9 Pat Morris (top), Peter Clayton (bottom); 10 Peter Clayton (top left), Aldus Books (top right); 12 Mansell Collection (top left), Aldus Books (top right), Sonia Halliday (center); 13 Sonia Halliday (top), Athens Museum (center & bottom); 14 British Museum (top), Michael Holford/British Museum (center & bottom); 15 British Museum (top); 16 D. A. Courtney (top), John Freeman/British Museum (bottom); 17 Robert Harding Associates (top left), British Museum (top right & Center), D. A. Courtney (bottom); 18 British Museum; 19 British Museum (top), Michael Holford (center); 21 Egyptian Tourist Office (top left & right), T. Rowland-Entwistle (bottom); 22 British Museum (top, center & bottom); 23 Universitets Oldsaksamling, Oslo (top & bottom), Statens Historiska Museum, Stockholm (center); 24 Sonia Halliday (top left), Michael Holford (bottom); 25 Sonia Halliday (top); 27 British Museum (top right & left, center right & left), Peter Clayton (bottom left), Michael Holford (center); 28 Enrico Tricarica (top), Sonia Halliday (bottom); 29 Robert Harding Associates (top), Studio Fotografico Begotti (bottom); 30 Peter Clayton (top), Novosti Press Agency (bottom); 31 Danish Tourist Board (top), William MacQuitty (bottom); 32 William MacQuitty (top), Peter Clayton (center & bottom); 33 William MacQuitty (center & bottom); 34 National Monuments Record, London; 35 Photoresources/C. M. Dixon (top & bottom); 36 William MacQuitty (top right, center, & bottom); 37 William MacQuitty (top & bottom); 38 Jim Gill: Seaphot (top left), Sonia Halliday (bottom right), Wasavarvet/Statens Sjöhistoriska Museum, Stockholm (center); 39 Athens Museum (top right); 40 Yigael Yadin (bottom); 41 Yigael Yadin (center), Israel Tourist Office (bottom); 42 London Museum; 43 London Museum; 44 British Museum (top left), French Tourist Office (top right), London Museum (bottom); 45 Ken Merrylees (top), Fishbourne Archaeological Trust (bottom); 46 Mansell Collection (top), Michael Holford (bottom); 47 Robert Harding Associates (top), Department of the Environment, London (center), C. R. Warn (bottom).
Artwork: W. Francis Phillipps, Stobart Sutterby, Faulkner/Marks Partnership, Joyce Tuhill/Linden Artists. Cover: John Sibbick
Picture Research: Penny Warn and Jackie Newton